D1307368

Fever at the Poles

written and illustrated by Stephen Aitken

visit us at www.abdopublishing.com

Published by Magic Wagon, a division of the ABDO Group, 8000 West 78th Street, Edina, Minnesota 55439. Copyright © 2012 by Abdo Consulting Group, Inc. International copyrights reserved in all countries. All rights reserved. No part of this book may be reproduced in any form without written permission from the publisher.

Looking Glass Library™ is a trademark and logo of Magic Wagon.

Printed in the United States of America, North Mankato, Minnesota.
052011
092011
 This book contains at least 10% recycled materials.

Written and Illustrated by Stephen Aitken
Edited by Stephanie Hedlund and Rochelle Baltzer
Cover and interior layout and design by Abbey Fitzgerald

Library of Congress Cataloging-in-Publication Data

Aitken, Stephen, 1953-
  Fever at the poles / written and illustrated by Stephen Aitken.
    p. cm.
  Includes index.
  ISBN 978-1-61641-671-3
  1. Arctic regions--Climate--Juvenile literature. 2. Sea ice--Arctic regions--Juvenile literature. 3. Climatic changes--Environmental aspects--Arctic regions--Juvenile literature. I. Title.
  GB2595.A38 2012
  551.6911--dc22
                              2011001873

Contents

Polar Meltdown

Temperatures all over the world are rising due to climate change. This is melting the ice in Earth's freezers.

Climatologists are scientists who study climates. They are shocked at the rise in temperatures in the North and South Poles. The Arctic is warming twice as fast as the rest of the planet. Some places in Antarctica are warming five times as fast.

Arctic Sea and Ice

In the Arctic Sea, ice is melting. Seals use ice to move from one hunting area to another. Seal pups are born on floating ice. Seals are dropping in number as the Arctic waters warm.

6

HOT FACT: Whales are appearing farther north than they have ever been seen before because of warmer waters and less ice.

Walruses usually feed in deep waters by riding on ice floes. Now, they are gathering on the shore because there is less ice. Too many walruses in one place could wipe out food sources.

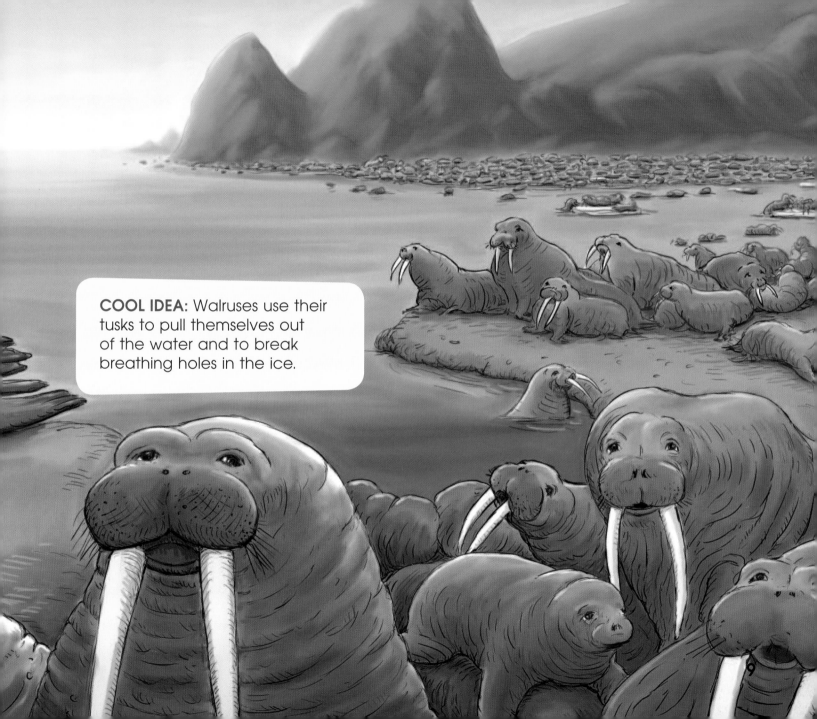

COOL IDEA: Walruses use their tusks to pull themselves out of the water and to break breathing holes in the ice.

In the Frozen North

Caribou feed on plants in the Arctic. But it is hard for them to reach their food. Insects are keeping caribou herds on the move with little time to feed. More rain is making an icy layer on the ground, covering their food.

HOT FACT: Less than 700 Peary caribou remain in the wild today.

11

The Arctic fox is also having a hard time surviving. In some countries, this fox has almost disappeared. With warmer temperatures, the red fox is moving north and competing with the Arctic fox for food. Climate change could be the final blow for the Arctic fox!

Climate change is also changing migration patterns. Brant sea geese used to escape the cold Alaska winter by flying to Mexico. With less coastal ice, it is now easier for the geese to reach their favorite food. Some Brant geese choose to nest on the Alaskan coast now.

HOT FACT: Polar bears hunt seals from floating ice. Loss of ice is making it harder for polar bears to survive.

Problems in Penguin Paradise

In Antarctica, emperor penguins are built to survive the cold winters. But today there are only half as many as there were 50 years ago. This is because the warmer Southern Ocean produces less krill, the emperor penguin's favorite food.

chinstrap

Chinstrap penguins like ice-free waters. But Adélie penguins need the ice to survive. As air temperatures rise, the Adélie and emperor penguins are moving closer to the South Pole.

Adélie

emperor

19

The Antarctic mainland is the coldest place on Earth. It is also one of the driest. Only Antarctic hairgrass, moss, and a few tiny insects can survive there. Rising temperatures are causing new plants to pop up and change the very simple Antarctic ecosystem.

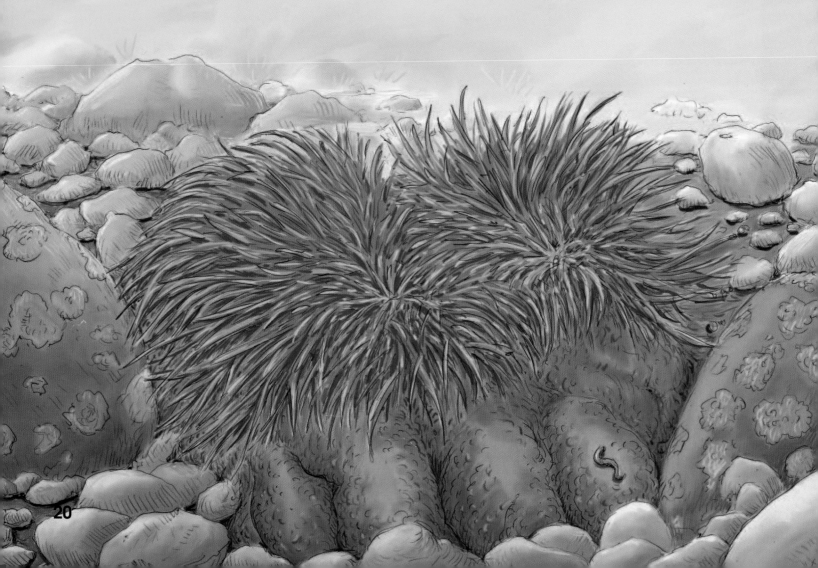

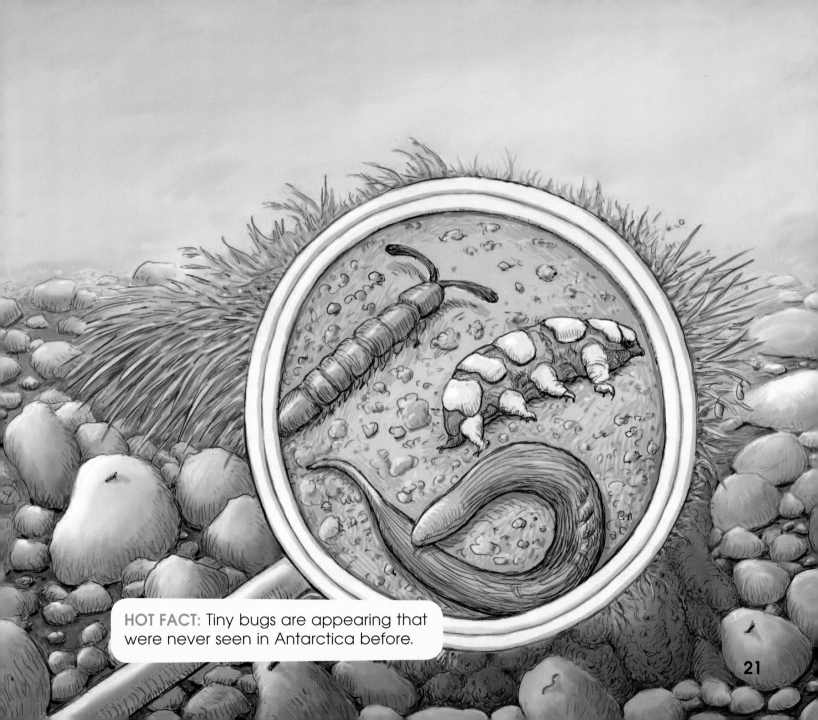

HOT FACT: Tiny bugs are appearing that were never seen in Antarctica before.

Antarctic Islands

The islands of Antarctica have a warmer climate than the mainland. Beetles, flies, nesting birds, and spiders can live there. More plants are appearing as the waters warm and air temperatures rise.

22

Many kinds of penguins live on the islands. The South Georgia pintail is the only freshwater duck in Antarctica. It has also adapted to the cold climate. More birds may start to appear as the temperatures continue to rise.

gentoo

macaroni

rockhopper

HOT FACT: Rats were accidentally brought to some islands and are wiping out bird populations. Scientists fear that warmer temperatures could lead to the arrival of more animals that upset the simple ecosystems.

25

Saving the Poles

Scientists have pulled up an ice core from the Antarctic ice sheet. It contains information about the climate of the last million years. We need as much information as possible to learn how to protect the plants and animals of Earth's poles.

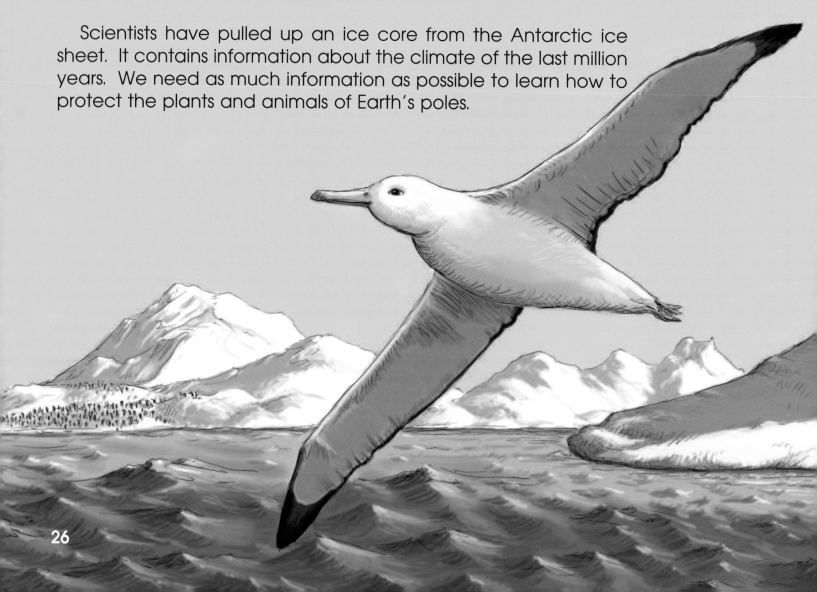

COOL IDEA: The albatross has a special beak that removes salt from seawater. This provides freshwater for long ocean journeys.

Did You Know?

Microscopic life is changing, too. Medicines that scientists have not yet discovered could be lost to science forever.

A walrus is heavier than a polar bear. But, it can move on land as fast as a man can run!

Many scientists think that by 2030 it will be possible to sail a ship across the Arctic Ocean in the summer.

Ringed seals are the most common Arctic mammals. They build snow-covered houses on the ice. But this is hard to do when the amount of snow is lower due to warmer temperatures.

Blue whales are the largest animal to ever live on Earth. They eat tiny floating plants and animals called plankton. Warmer sea waters produce less plankton. This means there is less food for these whales.

The loss of Arctic sea ice from 2003 to 2008 was equal in size to Alaska's entire land surface.

Dr. Know Gives Advice on Ice

Watching an ice cube melt can be much more exciting than you think. This two-part experiment will make your head turn – twice! At the same time you will see how water and ice act in polar oceans.

What you need:

A bowl	Ice cubes
Warm water	Food coloring

What to do:

1. Pour warm water into the bowl.
2. Drop in an ice cube and watch it closely as it melts.
3. Record the number of times it turns over on its side until there is no ice left.

Do you know why the ice cube turned over? The warm water made the bottom of the ice cube melt faster than the top. Soon the top was heavier than the bottom, so it tipped over.

4. Make colored ice cubes by putting food coloring in the water in the ice cube tray and freezing it.
5. Place several ice cubes in the bowl with warm water.
6. Record how long it takes for color to leave the bottom of the ice cubes.

The color allows you to see that cold water is heavier than warm water. This makes it sink to the bottom. However, very cold water freezes into ice, which is lighter than water. That's why ice cubes float. Isn't water weird?

What Can You Do?

The change in Earth's temperature is almost totally due to human activities. People burning oil and gas for cars, trucks, and buses releases gases that trap heat on Earth. The power used to create electricity and other forms of energy adds to the problem. Here are a few things you can do to help keep the temperature from rising more!

Wasted electricity, especially if it is non-renewable energy, adds to climate change.

A television that is on with nobody watching is wasting electricity. Turn it off.

Check to see if electrical appliances not being used are still plugged in and drawing power. Unplug them!

A computer that is on with nobody using it is wasting electricity. Turn it off.

Plug your electrical devices into power strips. That way you can flick the power strip switch to "off" when they are not in use.

Be an electrical ghost buster by getting the phantom electricity out of your home.

Glossary

climate - the weather and temperatures that are normal in a certain place.

ecosystem - a group of living and non-living things that interact with each other in a given area.

ice core - a tube of ice pulled from deep down in an ice sheet or glacier.

ice floes - floating, flat sheets of sea ice.

ice sheet - a thick layer of ice covering a large area of land.

krill - tiny, shrimplike animals that live under the polar ice, providing food for whales, fish, and sea birds, including penguins.

mammal - a group of living beings. Mammals have hair and make milk to feed their babies.

migrate - to move from one place to another, often to find food.

non-renewable energy - a source of power that can run out of supply, like oil or coal.

plankton - tiny animals, plants, and bacteria that drift on the ocean waters.

Web Sites

To learn more about climate change, visit ABDO Group online at **www.abdopublishing.com**. Web sites about climate change are featured on our Book Links page. These links are routinely monitored and updated to provide the most current information available.

Index

WITHDRAWN

For Every
Individual...

Renew by Phone
269-5222

Renew on the Web
www.imcpl.org

For General Library Infomation
please call 275-4100